A TRA
SEL

Translated from the Hungarian, with an Introduction
by Michael Castro and Gábor G. Gyukics

A TRANSPARENT LION

Selected Poems of Attila József

With a Preface by Dezső Tandori

GREEN INTEGER
KØBENHAVN & LOS ANGELES
2006

GREEN INTEGER BOOKS
Edited by Per Bregne
København / Los Angeles

Distributed in the United States by Consortium Book
Sales and Distribution, 1045 Westgate Drive, Suite 90
Saint Paul, Minnesota 55114-1065
Distributed in England and throughout Europe by
Turnaround Publisher Services
Unit 3, Olympia Trading Estate
Coburg Road, Wood Green, London N22 6TZ
44 (0)20 88293009

(323) 857-1115 / http://www.greeninteger.com

First Green Integer Edition 2006
English language translation copyright ©2006 by Michael Castro and
Gábor G. Gyukics
Introduction ©2006 Michael Castro
Preface ©2006 by Dezső Tandori
Back cover copy ©2006 by Green Integer
The translators and publishers would like to thank the following
foundations and organizations for their help in support of this publication:
Hungarian Translators House Foundation; Mihaly Tancsics Press
Foundation; The Ministry of Hungarian Cultural Heritage;
Sándor Petőfi Museum of Literature.

Design: Per Bregne
Typography: Kim Silva
Cover photograph: Attila József

LIBRARY OF CONGRESS CATALOGING IN PUBLICATION DATA
Attila József [1905-1937]
A Transparent Lion: Selected Poems
ISBN: 1-933382-50-3
p. cm – Green Integer 149
I. Title II. Series. III. Translators

Green Integer books are published for Douglas Messerli
Printed in the United States on acid-free paper

Contents

Attila József: Translator's Introduction   9

My Attila József, Our Attila József   23

Drunk on the Tracks (1922)   29

Winter (1922)   30

Rebellious Christ (1923)   31

Art Amongst Men (1924)   34

It's a Nice Summer Evening (1924)   35

It Isn't Me Who Shouts (1924)   37

We Are Now At the
Beginning of Creation (1924)   38

With Pure Heart (1925)   40

My Land I Bear (1925)   41

My Mother Died (1925)   42

Attila József (1925)   43

A Transparent Lion (1926)   45

My Fingers Possess Your Hair (1926)   46

Attila József (1927)   47

O Europe (1927)   48

Place Your Hand (1928)   49

The Seventh One (1932)   50

Forlorn (1933)   53

Yellow Grass (1933)   55

Freight Trains Shunt (1933)   56

The Sun Still Smoulders...   58

Elegy (1933)   59

My Homeland...   63

At the Edge of the City (1933)   64

The Water Turns Mushy...   69

Ode (1934)   70

The Ice on the Lake...   77

Consciousness (1934)   78

The Leaves on the Tree (1934)   84

Late Lamenting (1935)   85

Ah, Almost (1936)   88

That Pretty Woman from
the Past (1936)   89

Enlighten (1936)   91

I Cannot Find...   93

It Hurts Deeply (1936)   94

I Don't Belong to Anyone...   99

By the Danube (1936)   100

They Say (1936)   104

Our Poet and His Time (1937)   105

Rise From the Tide (1937)   108

An Ancient Rat Spreads Disease (1937)   110

I Saw Something Beautiful (1937)   112

The Shadows (1937)   114

To Those I Pretended Happiness (1937)   115

To a Poet (1937)   116

You Know There is
   No Forgiveness (1937)   117

In a Light White Shirt (1937)   120

If You Won't Press… (1937)   122

Thus, I Have Found
   My Homeland (1937)   123

For My Birthday (1937)   125

Nothing…   128

Attila József: Translator's Introduction

Attila József, regarded by many as Hungary's greatest twentieth century poet, was born in Budapest, April 11, 1905, and died, an apparent suicide, December 3, 1937, in Balatonszárszó, Hungary, by throwing himself under a train.

During József's short life he published seven books of poetry: *Szépség koldusa* (The Beggar of Beauty), 1922; *Nem én kiàltok* (It Isn't Me Who Shouts), 1925; *Nincsen apám, se anyám* (Got No Father, No Mother), 1929; *Döntsd a tőkét ne sivánkozz* (Ruin the Capital, Do Not Cry), 1931; *Mevetánc* (Bear Dance), 1931; *Külvárosi éj* (The Outskirts of Night), 1932; and *Nagyon fáj* (It Hurts Deeply), 1937. After his death, some seventeen additional collections of selected poems were issued by various Hungarian publishers. In addition, seven anthologies of writings dedicated to Attila József by other writers (including poems, articles, reviews and memoirs) have appeared in Hungary. Other Hungarian works include fifteen biographies and memoirs, twelve critical studies, and forty-one monographs and other scholarly works. At least six monographs and critical studies relating to József can be found in English, French, German and Italian. His poetry has been translated into over fifty languages. And the poets and translators are still at work.

The present work selects poems from among the earliest he produced in his teenage years to those representative of his entire career up until his death in 1937. Some of his best known works are here, like "By the Danube," "It Isn't Me Who Shouts," and "It Hurts Deeply," while others are included that are not currently available in English translation. We have tried to represent as faithfully as possible the great range in style, subject matter, and attitude in József's work. The images are his. We have also tried to capture as closely as possible the rhythmic patterns of the poems we've translated. Where we've employed rhyme, we've followed the rhyme schemes in the originals. Our goal has been, of course, not to create exotic curiosities, but poems that can stand on their own in English while representing their maker well.

József lived a difficult life marked by severe poverty, loneliness, and depression. In many ways his struggle for personal stability paralleled that of his native Hungary during an uncertain and turbulent period of the twentieth century, nominally between wars. József wrote about both the personal and the societal uncompromisingly, with vivid, often startlingly surreal imagery, or with stark confessional realism. Always he wrote in intense emotional tones that swung between despair and hope. Ted Hughes, writing of Attila József, has referred to the "unconsolable howl of his exposure to what had happened and continued to happen...counterpointed by a strange elation, a savage sort of elation or even joy."

József invigorated old poetic forms with a new freedom, orchestrating his poems with fresh rhythmic patterns that seemed, simultaneously, timelessly familiar. Like Hungary's great musical genius of the century, Béla Bartók, he was influenced by folk music's rhythms as well as their metrical patterns. But he was also influenced by dadaist and other modernist ideas sweeping Europe. He ultimately found a poetic voice that synthesized these opposing tendencies into something fresh and new and, for many, timeless. His poems are characterized by an intensity bordering on desperation, and could include, often in the same poem, both the grit of the street and the glory and wonder of the cosmos. Again, the testimony of Ted Hughes: "Every part of his nature seems to cooperate in each poem. But the truly arresting thing is the last-ditch urgency under which this cooperation happens. It is both genuinely desperate and irresistibly appealing. . . Bleak options, eternal perspectives, cleanly confronted."

József was abandoned by his father at the age of three and separated with his two sisters from his mother that same year. For the next four years he was raised on a farm by a poor foster family, who denied him his given name Attila, called him Pista (Steve), and put him to work as a swineherd. His foster father beat him constantly. At the age of seven he was reunited with his mother. She was an emotionally and physically fragile woman. Nevertheless, she struggled to support herself and her children, working sporadically as a washerwoman and domestic. Attila and his two sisters often went hungry. He performed odd jobs when he could get them, or stole food or firewood to help feed the family. In 1918, his sister Jolán's husband, a lawyer, became Attila's guardian and he was placed in a boarding school where his innate brilliance soon became apparent. A year later, in 1919, his mother died. The loss of his mother and father in his childhood figures prominently in his poetry, haunting it with a sense of abandonment that becomes a metaphor for the human condition.

Despite his anguished anger at their loss, Attila at the same time often idealizes his mother and father in his poetry. In his great poem, "By the Danube," he writes, "Food came sweet from my mother's mouth, / from my father's came the beauty of truth,"—this despite a youth characterized by constant hunger and the absence of his father forever after his third year. He describes his father in the same poem as "half-Székely, half Rumanian, or perhaps he was entirely that." Székelyland is a region of Transylvania with a large Gypsy population. Such hints found in his writings have led many contemporary Hungarians, especially those in the Gypsy intellectual community, to claim he was part Gypsy. While no conclusive evidence exists, these claims underscore Attila József's universal appeal.

Attila, with the support of his sister and brother in law, continued his schooling and began to express himself in poetry. In 1922 his first book of poetry, *Szépség Koldusa* (A Beggar of Beauty), was published. Thus began his literary career. But his successes were not without grief. The free thinking evident in his poems caught the attention of the witch-hunters of the semi-Fascist, anti-Semitic Horthy regime. He was suspected, incorrectly, of being in league with leftist and Jewish forces seeking to undermine "Christian" Hungary. He was tried for "blasphemy" in 1924 for his poem, "Rebellious Christ." He was found guilty and sentenced to eight months in prison. The sentence weighed heavily on him until it was reversed by an appeals court. In 1925, as a student at the University of Szeged, he published his second collection of poems, *Nem én kiáltok* (It Isn't Me Who Shouts). But a powerful professor, Anton Horger, outraged by his poem "With a Pure Heart" (subsequently regarded as among his greatest works), "advised" him away from the teaching career to which he aspired, and he dropped out.

Over the next several years he pursued studies in Vienna, Paris, and Budapest, continuing to write and publish poems earning the respect of poets and critics alike. In 1927 his inclusion is announced on the cover of *L'Esprit Nouveau*. No 1. along with Hans Arp, Tristan Tzara, F. T. Marinetti, Kurt Schwitters, Piet Mondrian, Fernand Leger, Mohaly Nagy et. al. He survived on short-lived jobs—hawking newspapers, working as a janitor, a book salesman, a bank clerk—and by relying on the kindness of family, friends and admirers. He never achieved anything close to financial stability.

He joined the Communist Party in 1930 only to be expelled from it in 1933. He began psychoanalysis in 1931, which he continued on and off for the remaining years of his life as his psyche became increasingly fragile. This fragility was exacerbated in the 1930's by a series of intense love affairs that ended badly. He never married. Through this difficult period in a difficult life he continued to write poetry, often brilliantly. In 1936, he became co-editor of *Szép Szó* (The Luminous Word), a humanist left-liberal journal intended to counter the growing influence of right wing extremism in Hungary. In addition to increasing his visibility on the Hungarian intellectual scene, *Luminous Word* was a place where he could publish his own poems, enabling a wider audience to become aware of his genius. Nevertheless, his health and emotional condition continued to worsen.

He was hospitalized twice for acute depression, and finally for an apparent psychological breakdown that was treated with drastic psychopharmaceutical therapy, including insulin shock treatments. On April 11, 1937, the last birthday he was to experience, Attila József wrote in his journal:

> Thirty-two years ago—more precisely at 9 P.M. on April 11, 1905, according to the penitentiary records—after a judiciary detention of nine months I was sentenced to lifelong

correction in a workhouse on counts of sedition, espionage, betrayal of secrets, indecent exposure, vagrancy, repeated scandalous behavior and pathological prevarication. My appeal for pardon having been rejected, I was transferred into the world of incorrigible criminals. The authorities concealed the ineffectualness of the investigation by presenting evidence obtained under torture which, I can testify, lasted an eternity. I maintained my innocence in vain; the court accepted the results of the investigation and my forced confession, as the basis of its decision.

József was writing a kind of spiritual epitaph, summarizing his life, and the life of his soul, as an imprisonment of eternal torment, which he expressed in his "forced confession," his poetry. He has subsequently been called a "genius of pain." Upon his release from the hospital, he was placed in the custody of his sister. It was thought that living with her family in the countryside would be helpful and, despite missing the literary action of Budapest, he appeared to be getting better before he suddenly threw himself to his death, or stumbled, under the wheels of a speeding train.

Though early in his career Attila József had the friendship and support of more established writers who eventually became prominent like Gyula Juhász, József Erdélyi and Gyula Illyés, and he was published by one of the giants of his age, Mihály Babits, Attila József was very much a literary outsider throughout his life. When Babits seemed to fend off his overtures for a closer relationship, József foolishly mocked him insultingly in a poem. Possibly as a result, he never could crack the literary establishment. His career was undercut in other ways as well. Many of his contemporaries scorned and rejected him because of exaggerated rumblings about his supposed communistic subversive leanings. Friends and acquaintances report he could be a difficult person. He was often perceived as too aggressive or arrogant, especially for one so young. His financial desperation could push him to demand loans or handouts in ways that grated on people. He never won a major Hungarian award during his lifetime.

Nevertheless, many, even among his harshest critics, recognized his genius. Many in the literary world tolerated his shortcomings because they understood he was special—a unique talent, a writer operating at a higher level. His sudden death in 1937, when he was only thirty-two, shook the literary world, as if they had known all along they had an unrecognized giant among them. Their mourning, within a year or two, spread to the nation at large, and Hungary continues to mourn his loss and to cherish his poetic greatness. Today, one of Hungary's most prestigious literary awards is named after him. His birthday, April 11th, is celebrated annually as Hungary's National Poetry Day.

József's poetry speaks both from and to the sense of individual isolation, and the social and spiritual poverty of the modern condition; and at the same time he speaks to the twentieth century's hopes and longing for something transcendently better. His work is both personal and social in its focus, often simultaneously. As he writes in one of his poems entitled, "Attila József," "his decay was nationwide."

When I discussed Attila József's unique appeal to Hungarians with the young poet, Ádám Dukay

Nagy, as we sat in Grinzingi, a popular wine bar in downtown Pest, he replied that Attila József's reputation rests on several pillars. First, he transcended politics—the Left could embrace him as one of their own, pointing to the time he spent close to socialism and communism and to the many calls for social improvement found in his work; but the Right, starting with the quasi-fascist and anti-Semitic literary establishment to which he would never bow, also could embrace him as a pure poetic genius after his death. Second, he came out of the people. He was not an aristocrat like many of the great Hungarian literary figures. Third, Hungarians have responded strongly to the music of his verse, rhythms that speak directly and powerfully to people of all strata of society and subsequently have inspired countless adaptations in folk, blues, jazz, and modern musical idioms. Fourth, the language and meanings of his poetry are not obscure, but direct and available to everyone, not just an educated or literary elite. And fifth, his naked pain could be felt and connected with by everyone—the pain of twentieth century humanity.

József's life and work embody the pressures and possibilities of the world he inhabited—a world lacking adequate guidance, ravaged by poverty, a world that was isolating, fast-moving, violently self-destructive, unpredictable—yet with unlimited potential and unlimited longing for transformation and transcendence. His writings spoke to his times with unprecedented frankness and inspiration, and continue to speak to our own.

MICHAEL CASTRO, 2004

My Attila József, Our Attila József

Nowadays, in the region where Hungary can be found, that this is "my" or "mine" or "us" or "ours" can hardly be said about anyone or anything. But we can certainly say all these about Attila József. "Hungary" – I said, instead of saying "my homeland." (Forgive me for all these concepts. Attila József is very much a UNIVERSAL-POET, but "OUR HOMELAND" owns him as well! To say this might sound weird after the century of Rilke, Kafka, and Eliot. With them Attila József has a loose, but, seen in depth, an obviously flowing connection–on the surface, I repeat, he doesn't have much in common with the tendencies, and with those who determined these tendencies, of the era: Joyce, Proust, Musil. Yet he is an equivalent-luminary.) I can't say "my homeland" because the homeland of the poet is that certain Poet's-land, whether it's Wittgensteinian philosophy, or a more sociological chain of doctrines, or "Zen"—it is to such a homeland where you must go to understand the poet, says Goethe.

Attila József could remain in his homeland in our homeland and become a perceptive poet of the universe. A seer of the universe—without physically seeing the world. Okay, he visited Paris, Vienna, etc. Despite his young age I could say, but, on the other hand, rather because of his preserved youth, his small and--large scale perception of the universe is unparalleled. Neither the tragic death nor the inhuman "system" which later took advantage of his ideas—his naivety, which willingly or unwillingly supported the culture more then others did, destroyed him. His shouting, shrieking voice didn't become the subject of stuffy psychology; his human truth didn't drown in the pulp and in the dust of the changing trends, styles and fashions of the decades. His clear view didn't turn to a crazy-vision, the discipline of his rage makes one feel calm, and not only is it fantastic that today's young Hungarian lyricists "begin from/with him" from zero, or else from their own one, plus his milestone, not only that "communal" fact is amazing but in almost every city, small town and village he has a street, a square, a "housing project" named after him.

These are external factors. For here no one can sit down by the bank of our main river, the Danube, without seeing his melon rind swim by; no one can think about the future without wishing for a computer, a trip to China, and also a fireplace, a family, —I double back—let's provide bread and work for everyone, and no one can say without him: calm down, relax, you don't have to be a hero if it isn't possible.

Without him no one can pray to God—to any God, no one can believe in matter and soul, I could make a long-long list of what we can't do without him. Attila József, or J.A., cannot be avoided. He is fiery like the Sun, he said this about himself and this is what the Sun suggests to me:

THERE IS NO TURNING BACK!

(The Sun)

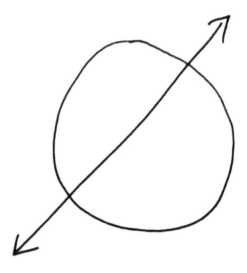

This is how I'm joking: isn't he the one who said
that, the Sun? J.A., for example inspires me, and
probably others, "us" too, to create such contra-
dictory clean things in an age, in a land, where I
can't say with "pure heart" that my homeland is
necessarily your homeland or that your homeland

is our homeland: where "our laws are still war-like"…I will stop right here, because whatever I say I can say only with his words. And I write "he" in lowercase, He wouldn't want it otherwise. We shortened him, he became J.A.—but his story is a poetry-forever long history, yes, he is History himself: and its truest breathing place: the count-less places of his many efforts. One doesn't neces-sarily have to be a hero, but to be working is a must. And it's good too. Let's make it possible. In this free flowing work process J.A. the poet, our emblem, will find a home. His poetry is difficult to translate because his fixed forms are connected to the essence of the subject, and because his grammatical wonders (however puritanical they are) belong to him. Yet I believe in the success of this book and that his voice will reach into the soul and will cause revelations.

DEZSŐ TANDORI
POET LAUREATE OF HUNGARY

Drunk on the Tracks

A drunk man lies on the tracks,
his left hand holds his bottle
and he snores. He sleeps in the chill of dawn.
Now, the Night trots away down the road.

His tousled hair is softly adorned
with weedy trash left by the evening wind,
the Sky sprinkles a divine frost upon him,
he doesn't move, his chest heaves though, he's alive.

His right fist, like a crosstie, is clenched tight;
he sleeps, as on his mother's lap long ago.
His clothes are ragged. He's still young: a mere lad.

The Sun isn't waking, the sky has turned ash-gray.
A drunk man lies on the tracks
and from afar, the earth slowly begins to rumble.

1922

Winter

A great great fire should be struck,
to warm the people up.

Throw everything on—antique, junk,
cracked, broken, even what is new and intact,
toys, —oh, a happy game of tag!—
and throw gustily everything on it that is beautiful.

The hot flame would sing to the sky
and everyone would hold hands as fellow countrymen.

A great great fire should be struck,
because the city, the groves are frosted;
tear off the handles from the frozen pantries
and strike them, to give lots of—lots of heat.

That fire, oh, ow! should be struck,
to loosen the people up!

1922

Rebellious Christ

"You, oh Lord, do not be Goodness,
do not be anything else, but the Righteous Lord!
Give us more bread, but don't let the rose
vanish.

Or don't just stay in your old Cosmos palace,
come out, see what your servant is doing—
your Life-cloak wouldn't be washed down to rags by
man's curses.

It was easy for you to break the thorn off with
    your hand,
you could still learn from me, my Lord—
I break it and I won't have supper, only a furlong
of land.

Yet I'm maintaining your land
and I'm already one huge aching spine—
I've bent down too much, don't tell me now
that I misunderstand.

Long as I'm able, to my duty I'm bound,
though nettle-stung bruises sit on my palm;
and if a storm comes, like a decaying tree
I'll stand my ground.

But loan me your cloak against the wind's blast.
Curse and rain cannot reach you:
You own a nice, noble palace and your legs
run fast.

In my work you don't pay me well at all,
my bed is cold against my body; Earth has
transmuted your golden words into hollow, gross
metal.

And in my work, Lord, I'm worth as much as
    You might,
in your great passion, be; and my soul
will be part of you soon, sprinkling the most beautiful
light;

it will become your eyes that see everything down here
    where it's hard…
What I'm saying is, you don't even have eyes yet,

You can't see now. I wish you'd become a righteous
God!"

Like a tired beast, his soul and body shiver.
Partners not getting much done, laugh at him—
and he stiffens, because he knows—evening falls on him
sooner.

From his huge, worn out soul, the words upward
   are wrung;
and he hangs his pale, faded heart out
like a hanged man, his voracious, gray
tongue.

1923

Art Among Men

She must have had wheels on her soles,
the dancer had rolled into our eyes,
she was simple, but shone, like a hummingbird.

Imagine a lanky demon swaying,
stretching above the swamp.
She'd bounced nicer than a young goat,
or like a rompish sheepdog whelp
when it runs and rolls on the lawn!

The year-round-sleepers would also happily
swing their hips with her!

I don't even know who was next to me,
as the cheers had whooped together inside us—
Then all at once the room grew cold
and us men, poor people, again
measured each other up, like strangers.

1924

It's a Nice, Summer Evening

It's a nice, summer evening.

Trains arrive and depart rumbling,
factories howl in fright,
the evening sooties sooty roofs,
a newshawk hawks under arc-lamps,
vehicles run by at random,
trams ringing in a huge procession.
Signs yell: you are blind,
walls wander into sidestreets
waving back a poster,
before you, behind you , all over—you see—
poster-faced men running, and—
one can see—behind large buildings
men
hallelujaing-shouting-groaning-cursing
gasping-coldly-cunningly-hastily
climbing high on men-ladders,
and one can hear, from the throats of angry avenues
whose veins are getting swollen,
how the tongue-tied clerks shriek,

the dilatory steps of workers walking home
as if all of them were wise old men
who have already nothing to do in the world.
One can hear the soft rotation of the wrists
    of pickpockets
and the chomping of a peasant from a bit further off,
who, at this very moment,
is skinning a large chunk out of his neighbor's land.
I, who am silent, can hear everything.
A wood worm whining in beggar-bones,
Women sniffing around—
but I came from afar,
I sit on my welcoming doorstep
in silence.

It's a nice, summer evening.

1924

It Isn't Me Who Shouts

It isn't me who shouts, it's the world that rumbles,
beware, beware, 'cause satan's gone crazy,
flatten yourself to the bottom of clear springs,
smoothen yourself into a sheet of glass,
hide behind the light of diamonds,
among bugs under the rocks,
oh, hide yourself in a freshly baked loaf,
you poor, poor…
Ooze into the ground with fresh rain showers—
in vain you soak it all into yourself,
you can wash your face only in others.
Be a tiny edge on a lone grassblade
and you'll be more than the axis of the world.

Oh machines, birds, branches, stars!
Our barren mother begs for a child.
My friend, my dear, loving friend,
either it's dreadful, or wonderful;
it isn't me who shouts, it's the world that rumbles.

1924

We Are Now at the Beginning
of Creation

Behold, the corpuscular man exists already,
lives and moves,
extends thoughts out of himself,
retracts them and extends them again,
to gain some space ahead.
'Til today he's struggled, now he saunters along,
but he's strenuous, and thus becomes ever stronger.

The stern law is gracious because of us.
We'll be efficient by tomorrow,
we'll swim, run, fly easily
and that's how it has to be,
then we won't care for anything, only
for the clean clothes of our soul,
for the virgin body of our yearned dreams,
for his body to be song and truth,
for his shape to be godlike,

this future multi-cellular man,
who will be thrown out of us,
who will be us,
the great Further-Creator,
for whom this world is dying.

1924

With Pure Heart

Got no father, no mother,
no god, no homeland,
no cradle, no shroud,
no kiss, no lover.

Last three days I haven't eaten
neither a lot, nor a morsel,
my twenty years is power,
I am looking for a buyer.

If no one wants it,
the devil will take it,
with a pure heart I will plunder,
if need be I will murder.

I'll be caught, I'll be gallowed,
with blessed earth I'll be covered,
& death spreading grass will grow,
on my oh, so beautiful heart.

1925

My Land I Bear

I'm Hungarian, but European.
Paris, love me, my land I bear,
my beautiful land, which awaits your kisses,
because here no one kisses her.

Moles live in her strong flesh—
Crows fly upon her full titties,
Paris, you are great and my land too
is dreaming about dancing cities!

Her rich tasting heart darkly dribbles,
the wind staggers away from her drunken reek—
from under its heavy, greasy soil
the cities' towering happiness speak.

If just one time she would realize her dreams,
Singing clearly with slim towers—
Paris, love me, my land I bear,
And I'll carry your kisses to her.

1925

My Mother Died

My mother died, now I don't know how to be
    with her;
she would patch my coat, she would observe
  how beautiful
    I am naked;
no one else has ever seen me naked!
The peasants have finished reaping, and are waiting
  for death on tiny benches—
bedbugs burn our dreams, our bowls are good only
  for hanging on the walls;
give me just a bit of butter for my bread.
But we want better meals, to become better,
more pairs of shoes by our beds, to become more.
The bridge slowly emerges out of the fog, bayonets
  guard the other side.

Here is the scissors , there is the fabric to be sewn—
  what are we waiting for?

1925

Attila József

Attila József, believe me that I love you so, I
   inherited this
from my mother, she was a blessed good woman,
see, she brought me into this world.
In vain we compare life to a shoe or to a dry cleaning
establishment, we like it for another reason after all.
Folks think they can redeem the world three times a day,
   yet they can't
even light a match; if things keep going this way,
I've had it with them.
It'd be nice to get a ticket to visit the Self,
it definitely lives inside you.
I bathe my thoughts in cold water every morning
so they become fresh and healthy.
If we plant diamonds under our hearts,
warm songs will grow.
Though there are people on horseback, in cars
   and airplanes,
still they are pedestrian. I'm lounging in the morning
   music of the larks,
though I've gone beyond the abyss.

Our true souls should be kept tidy, just like our Sunday
best, so they will be clean
for the holidays.

1925

A Transparent Lion

A transparent lion lives between black walls.
In my heart, when I call you, I wear ironed clothes;
I should not think about you, I must finish my work;
you're dancing.
I don't have a bite of bread to eat, yet I will live a
    long life.
It's been five weeks, and still I know nothing about you;
time's dashed away on blood-red wooden legs;
the roads cuddle up under the snow.
I don't know whether a man is allowed to love you;
silent black men play chess for your words that rang off
    ages ago.

1926

My Fingers Possess Your Hair

My fingers possess your hair, under your skirt
my heart hides in wonder
and the leaf of a calendar falls rustling.

My old threshold cries like a child
when you come, to come more.

An unruly mob of my old days,
gasping for breath, bites my ear —
why didn't you kiss us into it too?

And don't understand how pale, silly they are,
that your eyes cannot possess their light.

1926

Attila József

Was happy, pleasant, and perhaps stubborn
when they attacked him in his assumed right.
He liked to eat, he resembled God in some things.
He got a coat from a Jewish doctor,
and here's how relatives referred to him:
Don't-want-to-see-him-again.
He didn't find tranquility in the Greek
   Orthodox Church,
only priests.
His decay was nation-wide;

but, well, do not be sad.

1927

O Europe

O Europe, so many borders,
& at every border, murderers;
don't let me cry for the girl
who, two years from now, will give birth—

Don't let me to be sad,
because I'm European,
I'm buddies with free ranging bears.
Without freedom, I wither—

I write these poems to amuse you;
the sea has flooded the cape
and a fully set table swims
on the waves among the clouds—

1927

Place Your Hand

Place your hand
on my forehead,
as if your hand
were my own hand.

Guard me, as if
you would murder,
as if my life
were your own life.

Love me, as if
it were pleasant,
as if my heart
were your own heart.

1928

The Seventh One

Once you set foot on this earth,
Your mother gives you seven births!
Once in a blazing house afire,
once in an icy flood's cold mire,
once inside a loony bin,
once amidst waving wheat so thin,
once in cloister's hollow eye,
once among pigs in the sty.
All six cry, it's not enough, son,
Be yourself the seventh one!

If an enemy stands before you,
Have seven men who'd stand up for you.
One, who begins his day at leisure,
one who works his daily measure,
one who teaches gratis at his whim,
one who's thrown in the water to swim,
one who's the seed of a forest's growth of years,
one who's protected by his ancestor's tears.
But ruse or reproach won't get it done,—
Be yourself the seventh one!

If you'd go looking for a lover,
Have seven men try to find her.
One who for her word gives up his heart,
One who pays for his own part,
One who pretends to be a dreamer,
One who gropes her skirt to get her,
One who knows where her hooks can be found,
One who steps on her hanky on the ground,—
They all buzz like flies around carrion!
Be yourself the seventh one!

If you could afford to compile a tome,
Have seven men compose this poem.
One who builds a marble town,
One born asleep, his eyelids down,
One who charts the sky and knows it well,
One whose words can cast a spell,
One who sells his soul, trying to thrive,
One who carves up a rat while it's alive.
Two are brave and four are wise, son—
Be yourself the seventh one!

And if all this happened as was written,
Go to the grave as if you were all seven.
One who rocks on a milky chest,
one who grasps at dried hard breasts,
one who tosses away empty pans,
one who lends the poor his helping hands,
one who works like a man possessed,
one who stares at the Moon, obsessed;
You're already underground, my son!
Be yourself the seventh one!

1932

Forlorn

Slowly, Absorbed

In the end, man arrives
at a sandy, sad, moist plain,
looks around musing, and with his
clever head nods, hopes for nothing.

That's how, without delusion, I try,
looking around calmly.
Silvery axe-swishing plays
on the poplar's leaves.
My heart rests on nothing's branch,
its small body wordlessly trembles,
around it stars gather gently
and stare, stare.

In Iron-Colored Firmament

In an iron-colored firmament
a lacquery, cool dynamo revolves.
Oh, you silent constellations!
A word sparkles between my teeth—

Inside me the past falls wordlessly,
like a stone through space.
The silent, blue time sways away.
The edge of a sword sparkles: my hair—

My mustache, like a stuffed worm spreads
over my taste-escaped mouth.
My heart is heavy, the word goes cold.
But who can I call—

1933

Yellow Grass

Yellow grass on the sand,
this wind is a bony, old woman,
the puddle is a nervous cow,
the sea is silent yet tells a tale.

I croon my soft inventory.
That peddled coat is my country;
dusk crumbles on the hill;
my heart lacks the will to go on.

The coral reef of swarming time,
the dead world, the birch,
the tenement, the woman sparkle
through the flowing blue sky.

1933

Freight Trains Shunt

Freight trains shunt;
their pensive clatter
fastens light shackles
on the silent land.

The moon flies with such ease,
like a freed man.

The broken rocks
lie on their own shadows;
sparkle
to themselves,
they're on their spot
as never before.

What sort of giant night's
splinter is this heavy night,
falling upon us
like an iron splinter on the dust?

Sunborn desire!
If the bed admits a shade
would you stay
awake
through the night?

1934

The Sun Still Smoulders...

The sun still smoulders
over smothering mountains.
Behind the shirt of gloom
a meadow glimmers.

Elegy

Beneath a leaden sky plum,
condensed smoke,
like my soul, trails low
above the grim landscape.
Jerking not gliding.

You stiff soul, you soft image!
Following the heavy trace of truth,
behold yourself, your origin!

Here, where below the liquid sky,
upon the loneliness of lank firewalls,
the moody silence of need,
threateningly begging, dissolves the thick
layer of gloom on the ponderer's heart
and mingles it with
millions.

A whole race is molded here.
Everything in ruins.
A stiff dandelion opens its parasol in
an abandoned foundry yard.
On the faded stairs of tiny broken windows
the days ascend to moldy twilight.

Say—
are you from here,
where the somber longing never ends
to become like other wretched men
squeezed by this enormous age,
on whose faces every line is deformed?
Resting, where the greedy
moral order is guarded, protected
by shrieking, crippled
fences.

Can you recognize yourself?
Here the souls
petulantly wait for a beautifully designed, solid future
just as emptily as the melancholy, gloomy lots

everywhere dreaming
of nimble, noise weaving
tall houses. Glass shards dried in the mud
gaze at the suffering lawn with dull, stony eyes.

From the dunes, thimblefuls of sand
whirl below at random…and from time to time
blue, green or black flies flicker,
magnetized by man's scraps,
and rags
from the lands of wealth.
In her own way, setting a table, even here,
The credit burdened,
blessed mother earth.
Yellow grass thrives in an iron spittoon.

Do you know
the barren joy of this state of mind, that draws me,
that this land denies, and
the rich torment pushing me here?
For his mother, a child,
who's been beaten off to faraway corners,
will return.

Truly, you can smile, you can cry only here.
Here you can endure, only here,
oh soul! This is my home.

1933

My Homeland

My homeland, race and humanity
I do know my obligation,

like a mournful stranger at the end of the procession,
when someone gets buried with splendor.

At the Edge of the City

At the edge of the city, where I live,
during the crumbling dusk,
soot flies on soft wings,
like tiny bats,
and settles, like guano,
steadily, and thick.

That's how this age sits in our souls.
And like the heavy rain's
thick rags wash
the notched tin roofs' panes,
sorrow wipes the hardness
from our hearts in vain.

Blood can wash it too—that's how we are.
A new nation, another legion on old soil.

We differently pronounce the words,
the hair differently sticks to our heads.
But neither God, nor the mind, rather
coal, iron and oil;

the real substance created us,
only to dump us hot and recklessly
into the casting mold
of this awful society,
to make a stand,
in this eternal land, for humanity.

Following the priests, soldiers, citizens
we have have become the faithful guardians
of the law;
all human creations
and their intelligence
hum inside us like bass violins.

We have been indestructible,
since our solar system was created,
at least we haven't been destroyed up to now;
though many past tragedies are related
of how famine, guns, blind faith and cholera
left our homes devestated.

No destined winner has been
humbled and pushed around
as you were humiliated under the stars:
and thus we shot our eyes down:
and discovered the secret,
buried underground.

Look, how wildly the machine,
the dear beast, has rampaged!
Like the puddle's weakening ice,
fragile villages crack up and break,
and when the sky leaps and roars
the plaster walls of the cities shake.

So who calms the wild dog of the shepherd?
The landowner? Come on!—
The machine grew up with us.
Its childhood and our childhood are one.
For us, it's a meek animal. Now, call it!
Its name is on our tongue.

And yet we see already, that soon
you all will fall down on your knees
and pray to what is

merely your own property.
But only those who control and feed it,
are those that it obeys…

Thus, we are here, the children of the substance,
suspicious and together.
Let's lift up our hearts! They belongs to those
who lift them up, no matter.
Our collective will
can make each of us strong forever!

Up with the hearts, high above the factories!
Such sooty, great hearts' steep incline
of those only who saw and heard,
who saw the sun choke in its own smoke,
who heard the tunnels throbbing
in the world's deepest mines!

Up, up!…all around this divided world
the slatted fences stagger from our breath,
as if in a raging storm
they cry out, faint as if dead.
Blow them away! Up with the hearts,
Let them smoke overhead!—

Until we attain
our beautiful potential, order,
with which the mind can apprehend
the finite infinite,
the laws of creation outside,
& the instincts within.

This song whistles at the edge of the city.
The poet, your kin,
just stares, stares at it, the fat,
soft soot that falls and falls and drifts,
and settles, like the guano
steadily, and thick.

The word stammers on the poet's lips,
but he (this world's engineer of magic)
can see into the fully conscious future,
and can, inside himself, project
the same harmony you will,
finally, outside, erect.

1933

The Water Turns Mushy...

The water turns mushy, ice develops
and my sins assemble to death.

Ode

I'm sitting here on a shimmering precipice.
The light breeze
of the young summer, like the warmth
of a cherished supper, flies.

I make my heart get used to the silence.
It's not that hard—
what glided away, now swarms over here,
the head bends over and the hand
dangles

I watch the mane of the mountains—
the light of your forehead
sparkled by every leaf.
No one is on the road, no one,
I see how the wind
flutters your skirt.
And below the fragile hills

I see your hair inclining forward,
your soft breasts startling and
—while the Szinva creek runs away—
behold I see again, how the fairy laughter
springs on those round white stones,
your teeth.

2

Oh, how much I love you,
you who opened the universe
and the cunning loneliness
in the deepest cavern
of your heart.

You who part from me like the waterfall
from its own rumble, and softly run away,
while, among the peaks of my life,
near in the distance, I thunder, I scream,
struggling between the earth and the firmament,
that I love you, you sweet stepmother.

3

I love you like the child loves his mother,
like the taciturn caves their depth,
I love you, like enclosures love the light,
like the soul loves flame, like the body loves calm!
I love you, the way mortals love to live,
until they die.

I guard your every smile, motion and word,
like the ground guards fallen objects.
I etched you into my mind, like acid burns metal,
I burnt you in with my instinct,
you dear, beautiful image,
there your being fulfills every essence.

The moments march away rattling,
but you sit silently in my ears.
Stars ignite and fall down,
but you stand motionless in my eyes.

Your taste, like silence in the cave,
floats chilled in my mouth;
as with your finger round the waterglass,
delicate veins appear
luminously on your hand.

4

Oh, so what kind of matter am I,
that your glance carves and shapes?
What kind of spirit and light,
a vision worthy of amazement,
that I can wander through the haze of nothing-
ness
over your lush body's gentle slopes?

And as the verb enters into an opening mind,
I'm allowed to descend into its mysteries!…

The bloodvessels like rosebushes,
endlessly throbbing.
They carry the eternal current to reveal love
upon your face, to flesh out the blessed fruit of
your womb.

Through the sensitive ground of your stomach
many tiny roots embroider their tender yarn,
weave it into knots, loosen it,
the cells of your nectars collect their many legions
and the beautiful shrubs of your leafy lungs
whisper their own glory!

Eternal matter happily flows inside you
in the tunnels of the bowels,
and the excrement gains a rich vitality
in the wells of fervent kidneys!

Waving hills emerge,
constellations pulsate inside you,
lakes breathe, factories work,
millions of living animals bustle around,
bugs,
seaweed,
barbarity and goodness;
the sun shines, darkening northern light glooms—
in your substances,
the unconscious eternity wanders.

5

Like clotted scraps of blood
these words
float before you.
Existence stammers,
only the law is in clear speech.
Yet my diligent organs, born again
day by day, are preparing,
to become silent.

But until then they all shout—
You who were chosen from the crowd
of two thousand million,
you are the only one, you tender cradle,
strong grave, living bed—
allow me inside you!...

(How high is the morning sky at dawn!
Armies sparkle in their armors.
This great radiance hurts my eyes.
I am lost, I think.
I can hear my heart clatter and beat
above me.)

6

(Collateral Song)

(A train takes me, I go after you,
Perhaps today I will find you too,
Perhaps my blazing face will calm,
Perhaps, softly, your words will come:

The bath is warm, get in the water!
Use the towel to get dry!
Meat is frying, ease your hunger!
Your bed is right here where I lie.)

1933

The Ice on the Lake...

The ice on the lake is covered with slushy snow.

Consciousness

I

Dawn unties the sky from the world
and from her pure, soft voice
the bugs, the children
swirl out to the sunshine;
there is no mist in the air,
and shimmery lightness flutters!
The leaves are tiny butterflies
that flew upon the trees during the night.

II

I saw blue, red, yellow daubed
pictures in my dream
and I felt, this is order,
not a speck of dust messed them up.
Now my dream circulates through
my limbs like twilight, and the iron world is the order.
A moon wakes the day in me,
and if night arrives—a sun shines inside.

III

I'm skinny, I eat bread sometimes,
among these shallow, garrulous souls
I'm searching, without pay, for more certainty
than in the roll of dice.
Lush meat doesn't caress my mouth,
nor does any child my heart—
even a smart cat can't catch mice
inside and outside at the same time.

IV

Like a pile of chopped wood, the world
sprawls one piece on top of another,
each grips, presses, holds
one thing onto the other
and thus, every one is determined.
What doesn't exist, possesses a bush,
what will be, is the flower;
what exists, falls into pieces.

V

At the freight train station
I lay flat beside the tree's trunk
like a piece of silence: gray weeds
touched my mouth, raw, wierdly sweet.
Deadly still, I watched the guard,
intent on his senses, and his shadow
in the silent wagons jumping
stubbornly over the dewy coal

.

VI

So suffering is here inside,
but out there is the explanation.
Your wound is the world—burns, fiery.
And you feel the fever in your soul.
You're a prisoner, til your heart rebels—
You'll be free, if, for your pleasure,
you won't build the kind of a house
that a landlord takes over.

VII

From under the evening I looked
up into the cogwheels of the sky—
the loom of the past was weaving a law
out of the threads of glittering accident;
again, through the haze of my dream,
I looked up to the sky,
and I saw the seam of the law
kept coming unravelled all over.

VIII

Silence was listening—a clock struck.
You should visit your youth;
there among damp cement block walls
you can imagine a little bit of freedom—
I thought. And as I'm standing up,
the stars, the Big Dipper, sparkle
the way bars shine
above a silent prison cell.

IX

I heard the iron crying,
I heard the rain laughing.
I saw how the past split apart,
and how only illuisons can be forgotten;
and how I know nothing, but to love,
bending under my burdens—
why must we construct weapons
from you, golden consciousness!

X

The adult man is he who has no mother
and father in his heart,
who knows that life is something extra
thrown in beside death and, like a found object,
anytime it can be given back—
that's why he treasures it, he
who is neither god, nor priest,
neither for himself, nor to anyone.

XI

I did see happiness once, it was tender,
blonde and must have weighed four-hundred pounds.
Its curly smile tottered
on the rigorous grass of the farm yard.
It plunked down in a soft, lukewarm puddle;
it winked, grunted in my direction.
I still see how waveringly the light
fumbled among its ringlets.

XII

I live by the tracks. Lots of trains
come and go and I watch
how the shiny windows fly by
in the powdery-darkness.
This is how the lit up days
speed through the eternal night;
I'm standing in every cabin-light,
leaning on my elbow in silence.

1934

The Leaves on the Tree

The leaves on the tree
sway slowly.
They are all already warped, yellow
      and withered, soft.

A taciturn bird
twists among them.
As if the tree were
      its cage.

That's how my song walks,
sits hollow inside me,
and with it, its quivering shadow,
      the silence.

1934

Late Lamenting

I'm burning in eternal high fever
and you don't nurse me, mama.
Like an ethereal, loose girl, beckoned by a wave,
you stretched out by death's side.
I try piecing you back together out of soft
autumn landscape, and many lovely women;
but time is running out, I see,
        as the intense fire consumes me.

The last time I went to Szabadszállás, it was
the end of the wars
and in a tangled up Budapest
the stores stood empty, not even bread.
I lay down crosswise on the train-roof;
I brought potatos; had millet in a sack;
for you, your stubborn son, got chicken too,
        but you were already gone.

You took your self and your sweet breasts from me
And gave them to the worms.

You consoled and chided your son
and look how your pretty words were false, untrue.
You cooled my soup, blew it, stired it, and
said: Eat, grow big and strong for me!
Now your empty lips taste earth's greasy mold—
          you deceived me.

I wish I ate you!...You brought me
          your supper—did I ask?
Why did you bend your back doing laundry?
To stretch it out on the bottom of a box?
See, I'd be glad if you'd beat me once more!
It'd make me happy because I would hit back;
you are worthlesss! You don't want to live,
          and ruin everything, you shade!

You are more deceitful than any woman,
who cheats, and falsely promises!
Slyly you left your embodied faith,
born in pain out of love.
You Gypsy! What you gave me cajolingly,
you stole it all back at the last minute!
Hear me, mama! A child curses you—
          Stop me!

My mind is slowly clearing,
the legend is gone.
The child who hangs on to his mother's love,
relaizes how foolish he is.
Whoever is born to a mother is betrayed in the end.
Here, there, whichever way he tries to finagle—
Whether he fights, whether he reconciles,
    either way he dies

1935

Ah, Almost

Ah, love almost bursts me open.
Ah, fear almost crushes me down.
     Ladies, which of you would die
        with me in an embrace?

My summer is fast, and slow is my winter.
Who does autumn's square reveal?
     Who would fly away with me
        from the time of peeking scarecrows?

Bars of stars shine in the sky;
such a cave intelligence keeps me in!
     This universe, ladies,
        who will blow it up with me?

1936

That Pretty Woman from the Past

That pretty woman from the past I'd like to see again;
in her, ethereal, tender loveliness was reversed;
along the swale, when three of us leisurely wandered,
she happily and seriously walked in the light mire;
when she looked at me, I couldn't not tremble;
that pretty woman I'd like not to love.
What I want is to see her; in the sun, dreaming,
I have no plans, while she sits in the garden
and a closed book, like herself, lies in her hand;
around us, dense branches sigh in the autumn wind.
I would watch one time, as she hesitantly, slowly,
like one who conceives a plot in the rustling glade,
stands up, looks around, suddenly leaves and steps into
    the passage
which, behind the bushes of the garden, lurks, leading
    through the
distance with the farewell waving trees on both of
    its sides;

I'd like to see her, like a child longs to see his
    dead mother,
that pretty woman from the past, as she walks away in
    the light.

1936

Enlighten

Enlighten your children:
the gangsters are all human;
the witches—the mongers and hawkers, the hives,
—are yelping dogs, if not wolves!
They either bargain or philosophize,
but all, all change hope for money:
one sells coal, another love,
the third a poem like this.

And console them, if it's a consolation
for children, that that's the truth.
Or mumble them a new fable of
fascist communism—
for order is needed in the world,
and the order is because
children don't exist in vain
and what's good cannot be gratis.

And if a child opens his mouth,
gazes up at you, or weeps,
don't trust him, do not believe that
your principles will delude him;
look at the cunning baby:
crying to get pity, but while
he smiles at your breast,
he grows nails and teeth.

1936

I Cannot Find...

I cannot find words for myself.

It Hurts Deeply

Inside-outside
running from peeping death
(like a frightened mouse in the hole)

while you burn,
that's how you flee to a woman,
to her arms, lap, knees for shelter.

Not only the soft, warm lap,
not only desire cajoles you,
but the demand pushes you there too—

that's why everyone clings to her
who finds a woman,
until his lips turn white with need.

Double burden
and double treasure that one must love.
He who loves and cannot find a partner,

is as homeless,
is as helpless
as the beast relieving itself.

We have no other
shelter, even if you point the knife's
tip at your mother, you hero.

And see, there's a woman
who understands these words,
yet she pushed you away from herself.

I have no place now,
like this, among the living. My head rumbles,
orchestrating my trouble and pain,

like a child
who's abandoned, shaking
a rattle in his hand.

What should I do
for or against her? I'm not
ashamed to try figuring it out

because the world
expels those overwhelmed by the sun
and tormented by the dream.

Culture
falls away from me, like clothes
drop from others in happy love—

but where does she stand, staring
as I'm tossed about by death,
and do I have to suffer this alone?

The infant
suffers too, when a woman gives birth.
The double torture is eased by humility.

But for me
my painful song brings only money,
and shame comes to join me for free.

Help me!
You young boys, your eyes popping
where she wanders by.

Innocents,
shriek under boot heels,
and tell her: It hurts deeply.

You faithful dogs
scurry under tires
and bark at her: It hurts deeply.

Women, bearing your
burden, abort and
cry out to her: It hurts deeply.

Healthy humans,
fall, get yourself crushed,
and mumble to her: It hurts deeply.

All of you men,
tearing each other up for women,
don't suppress it: It hurts deeply.

Horses and bulls,
you who are dragging the yoke,
castrated, cry out: It hurts deeply.

Silent fishes,
bite the hook under the ice
and gasp at her: it hurts deeply.

All living things,
everything, that shivers with torture,
burn where you live, the gardens, the wilds—

and charred around her bed,
if she nods off,
stammer with me: It hurts deeply.

Let her hear it
as long as she lives. She denied him
out of pure pleasure

inside-outside,
from the man trying to escape,
she witheld the very last shelter.

1936

I Don't Belong to Anyone...

I don't belong to anyone, my word is a flying mold
I'm light and heavy like the cold.

By the Danube

I

I was sitting on the last step at the wharf,
I was watching how a melon rind swum away:
I hardly heard, submerged in my fate,
how the surface bubbled, how the deep kept quiet.
As if it had sprung from my heart,
the Danube was murky, wise and great.

Like muscles, when a man is working,
file, hammer, make adobe, dig,
that's how every wave and every motion
popped, stiffened and loosened,
like my sweet mother, rocked, told a tale
and washed all the city's dirty laundry.

And the rain began to drizzle.
But, as if it didn't matter, it stopped.
Yet, like one who watches a long rain
from a cave—I watched over the boundaries of the city:

The gaudy past was falling
like an apathetic, eternal, colorless rain.

The Danube just floated on.
And like a child on a fertile, day-dreaming mother's lap,
the waves were swaying playfully and laughing
   towards me.
They rumbled like gravestones,
staggering cemeteries in the flood of time.

II

I'm the type, that I watch for a thousand years
what I see all of a sudden.
The whole of time is complete in one second,
and a hundred thousand ancestors contemplate it
   with me.

I see, what they did not see, because they hoed,
murdered, embraced, they did what they had to.
They see, diving into the matter,
what I don't see, when one must confess .

We know about each other, like happines and sorrow.
Mine is the past, their's is the present.
We write a poem, they hold my pencil.
I feel them and remember.

III

My mother was Kun, my father half Székely,
half Romanian, or perhaps he was entirely that.
Food came sweet from my mother's mouth,
from my father's came the beauty of truth.
When I move, they embrace each other.
Because of this I'm sad sometimes;
this is the evanescence. I am made from this.
   "You'll see,
when we won't be around!…"—they address me.

They address me, because I'm already them;
That's why I'm strong in spite of my weakness,
remembering, that I'm more than the many,
because I'm all the ancestors back to the
   premordial cell—

I'm the Ancestor, who breaks apart to become more:
happily I change into my father and mother,
my father and mother also divide into two
and I expand to a fervent One!

I'm the world—everything, that was, is:
Many nations, which clobber each other.
The conquerers win with me dead
and the suffering of the conquered makes me suffer.
Árpád and Zalán, Werbőczi and Dózsa
Turkish, Tartar, Slovak, Romanian whirl
in this heart—today's Hungarians—
You owe a tender future to this past!

…I want to work. It's enough of a struggle
to admit the past. The Danube
is the past, the present and the future;
her soft waves embrace each other.
The battle, which was fought by our ancestors,
memory dissolves into peace;
and now we must finally put our house in order—
this is our work, and it's no easy task.

1936

They Say

When I was born, my hand held a knife,
     they say, it's poetry.
Yes, I grabbed a pen, because the knife wasn't enough:
     I was born as a man.

One in whom fiery devotion tearfully wanders,
     they say, that it's loving.
Oh, call me into your lap, weepy simplicity!
     I'm only playing with you.

I don't remember and I don't forget.
     They say, how can that be?
As if whatever I drop remains on the ground,—
     if I don't find it, you do.

I'm clogged by the ground and crumbled by the sea:
     they say, I die.
But one hears so many things,
     that to this I respond with silence.

1936

„Our Poet and His Time"

To Bertalan Hatvany

Behold a poem of mine.
This is its second line
"Our Poet and His Time"
sounds firm with letter T.
Nothing in it is flitting
as if it were the dust of anything—
as if the dust…

Nothing in it is flitting,
as if it were something: the world
swaying in expanding space
embarking upon its future
the way the branch sways and sea rumbles,
the way the dogs are howling
in the night…

Me, in the chair, that's on the ground
and Earth underneath the Sun,
the solar system and the jail
are revolving among the stars—

the universe wakes nothingness,
as, inversely, inside me
this very thought…

My soul is space: It would fly
to the mother, to great Space, high.
Like a balloon to its nacelle,
I tie it to my body.
It's neither real, nor is it a dream,
It's called: a sublimation of
my drive…

Come my friend, come look around
You are working in this world and
compassion's working inside you.
All the lies you tell are in vain.
Now, let this go, now, let that go;
watch the evening light with the evening
dissolve

As far as the slope stretches
the blood red stubble-field lies,
bluishly clotting. The tiny,
feeble lawn cries and bends down.

A cadaver-like lividity
sits softly on the happy hills.
Night's falling.

1937

Rise from the Tide

Terrify me, my god,
I need your anger.
Abruptly rise from the tide,
don't be dragged down by nothing's drift.

I, thrown by a horse,
and hardly visible from the dust,
I play with great torture's knives
that don't belong in the hearts of man.

I'm fiery, like the sun,
I lit such a flame—take it!
Shout: it's forbidden!
Strike my hand with your thunder.

And with your revenge or grace
convince me: that innocence is sin!
For being such an innocent
burns me more than hell.

I roll like the bite of a wild, yeast drooling
sea, when I lie alone.
I already dare everything,
but nothing results from nothing.

I hold my breath in order to die,
if you don't hit me with a mace;
and that's how I look into the eyes
of your manfaced absence!

1937

An Ancient Rat Spreads Disease…

An ancient rat spreads disease among us,
gobbles the unconsidered thought
that we had cooked up,
and runs from man to man.
That's why the drunk doesn't know,
when he kills his fancy in champagne,
that he gulps the empty soup of
disgusted little poor folks.

And because spirit doesn't squeeze
moist rights out of every nation,
a new odium startles the races
against each other. The oppression
croaks in choirs, flies light upon living hearts
as though they were carcasses—
misery oozes through the orbit,
like saliva on the faces of idiots.

On famine's stickpin stuck summers
hang their wings,
machines crawl in on our souls,

like bugs on sleepers.
Grateful devotion nestled within us,
tears roll into flames—the yearning
for revenge chases conscience
and vice versa.

Like a jackal that turns to throw
its voice up to the stars,
to our sky, where torments shine,
the poet shrieks in vain…
Oh, stars, you! Like rusty, rough
daggers around around, you have
been stabbed into me how many times—
(here one succeeds only to die).

Still I'm hopeful. And tearfully implore you
our beautiful future, don't be so dreary!…
I'm hopeful, for unlike our forbearers,
we won't be impaled today.
Soon the peace of freedom will arrive,
pain will become refined—
and we'll be forgotten finally
in the shade of silent pergolas.

1937

I Saw Someting Beautiful

I saw something beautiful, something sweet,
I imagined a tender rose
I gazed at it and, like a boulder,
reality tumbled down upon me.

But this boulder is only symbolic.
It's best if I speak directly...
This is how dutiful, edifying,
everyday problems teach us.

Behold, my instinct followed the
right path, when a man came in:
"he wants to turn off my lights"
rumbled in me like the sea.

The knife was on the table
—I was sharpening my pencil—
if I stab this fellow, I knew,
I would be getting even for everything.

I felt desperate. Now everywhere
will be dark and sad.
An animal can guard its home;
but this is another kind of war.

Grabbing a gun means weakness:
the enemy kills you, beats you and
your tenderness flies away.
In the State of Law, money is the gun.

Here and now, warfare is different.
The hero doesn't even draw his sword.
Banknotes ignite bombs' explosions
and shrapnel of little coins fly all about…

That's how I was thinking, I said
good day, and I drew away to the side,
and in the evening the gentle stars
smiled at me with the full moon.

1937

The Shadows

Shadows stretch up,
stars light up,
flames shoot up from coal,
and following undisturbed laws,
orbiting in space without pause,
your absence is spinning round in my soul.

Rumbling like sea, the night's percussion,
And the smell of floral passion
strangles my struggling heart asleep.
Lift me, release me from these depths.
I'm like a fish delighting in the nets
of your eyes plunging inside me deep.

1937

To Those I Pretended Happiness...

To those I pretended happiness—
smiles jerk me away nightly
from their sleeping faces,
like a moth in a storm.
Because that dead one who gave me birth,
who nursed me singing, came to get me.
Expanding the intellect like space,
songs recline in the silence.
Faith also shambles away.
My heart's love fades away.
What's revealed is how an empty thing,
the world's strife, roams inside
me, like a spirit, with the patience of existence.
My body dissolves, like fabric
that has been pulped by moths.

1937

To a Poet

You are loved: it's easy to see why,
you don't look for what's scary, when you must;
I reached up way too high for my sky
& grew heavy, that's why I sunk so fast.

I was born ten pounds, yet my mother survived.
That's why I have to wait around,
to be tolerated and revived
as a free soul on worldly ground.

Think you're lucky? I doubt it—my feeling,
is soon enough your standing will vanish,
or, begging for insults, kneeling
in wintery water you'll perish

(To my shame) I've succeeded
(at nothing, but the betrayal of man),
stuck eating stale bread
while God's body is shared from a pan.

1937

You Know, There is No Forgiveness

You know, there is no forgiveness,
though it's futile, all this sadness.
Be what you'd be: a man.
Grass will grow in your footsteps.

The sin won't be judged light,
you'll cry futilely with all your might,
but because you yourself are the proof,
give thanks, it's only right.

And don't promise, don't blame,
don't curse your soul and name,
don't conquer, don't yield,
don't join the army in the field.

Remain with the outsiders.
Leave the secrets to the hiders.
And don't ever, as a man,
snub your nose at mankind.

Remember, how you squealed
how futilely you appealed.
At your own truth telling trial
it was yourself that you revealed.

Fainting, you cried for your father:
for a man, even if there is no Father.
And you found how spoiled brats think
by talking to the clinic's shrink.

You believed in light words,
and paid for protection,
and look, see how no one's
defended your reputation.

At love, you were cheated.
Now you can't love, since you too have cheated.
Take aim at your empty heart
now, for a loaded weapon is needed,

or get rid of every notion
and hope for true devotion,
for a person you can trust,
like a dog, to believe in.

1937

In a Light, White Shirt

All that wasn't food
I chewed and spit out.
I've learned on my own what is good,
it hasn't mattered since the flood,
if the firmament or a soapbubble hovers about.

Like a little child, I know that happiness claims
only those who are allowed to play.
But I know many games
where only illusion remains
after all truth withers away.

The wealthy don't like who I am
Unless I live oh so squalidly.
And the poor, for me, don't give a damn.
Their comfort diminishes me as a man
where to love is ignominy.

I shall create my love...
my feet firmly on earth:
I shall go against the Gods —
my heart won't shiver—
in a light, white shirt.

1937

If You Won't Press...

If you won't press me to your bosom,
while you are happily dreaming,
as if I were your only possession,
you'll be grabbed by thieves; leaning
on the sofa, you cry out your confession:
how lonely and silly I am!

If you won't hold me with the vow
that you are happy because you live for me,
you can whisper to your hunched shadow,
when loneliness and fear tortures you.
But your love won't have a thread
if the stitches are all in shreds.

If you won't embrace me, devour me:
trees, mountains, waves will crush me.
I love you like a child,
and just as cruelly:
where you bathe in light, that place
I turn into darkness—and die.

1937

Thus, I Have Found My Homeland...

Thus, I have found my homeland,
the ground where my name is written faultlessly
above me by those who
would bury me, if they bury me.

This ground will shelter me, like a cash box,
for the twenty cent coin, the iron six
that lingered after the war,
(how unfortunate!) is superfluous.

As is the iron ring, with pretty words,
a new world, rights, land
etched in —yet our laws are still warlike
and golden rings are more grand.

I was alone for a long time.
Then, later, many came to see me.
You're alone, they said; though I'd have
gladly joined them if they asked me

I've lived and I existed in vain,
I've come to know this in my season.
They made me play the fool,
and my death doesn't have a reason.

Since I've lived amidst a cyclone,
I've tried to stand my ground.
It's ridiculous, I haven't wronged them
more than they've jerked me around…

The Spring is pretty, as is Summer;
Autumn is prettier, and Winter's special charm
is for those whose hope is for others'
hearth and family keeping them warm.

For My Birthday

Thirty-two I have turned today—
this poem by surprise came my way
               titty
               ditty:

the ultimate gift, with which
at this cafe I astonish
               myself
               myself;

my thirty-two years have been scattered
two-hundred a month I've never bettered.
               It's a trend
               my homeland!

I could've become a schoolmaster
instead of a fountainpen jester.
               needy
               weeny.

But I've gotten expelled, riot act read
at the university in Szeged
        mean
        dean.

His decision reached me fast and coarse,
my "no father" verse got his curse,
        he guarded
        the home hard

with drawn swords' scowls
he has summoned my soul's
        flame
        and name:

"You, as long as I have a word,
won't be teaching in this world"
        mutters
        and sputters

If that's Mr. Antal Horger's pleasure
that our poet shall not study grammar
                    a light
                    delight,

'cause it's beyond a high school education
I'll be teaching the whole nation
                    watch me
                    you'll see!

1938

Nothing

Nothing, nothing, nothing, nothing, nothing.
Let it be, not to be,
Let it be, not to be—
let's say: Edith.

Invisible, yellow little chicken
pecking the stars now.

Maybe dawn is breaking, maybe Budapest is on fire,
maybe make-up is melting
on the face of a sweating giantess.

Cars murmur, shutters trundle,
seas thunder, people flood.

That obnoxious house at the corner makes me angry—
it's like tinea on the face of a child.

Where I have just arrived.
either this morning is unknown, or this railway station
   is unknown.

I have no luggage.
I've forgotten something—I wish I could remember.
One: nothing.
Two: nothing.
Three: nothing.
It's just as strange as this railway station,
that there is nothing at all.

THE MARJORIE G. PERLOFF SERIES
OF INTERNATIONAL POETRY

This series is published in honor of Marjorie G. Perloff and
her contributions, past and present, to the literary criticism of interna-
tional poetry and poetics. Perloff's writing and teaching have been illumi-
nating and broad-reaching, affecting even the publisher of Green Integer;
for without her influence and friendship, he might never have engaged in
publishing poetry.

2002
Yang Lian *Yi* (GI 35) [China]
Lyn Hejinian *My Life* (GI 39) [USA]
Else Lasker-Schüler *Selected Poems* (GI 49) [Germany]
Gertrude Stein *Tender Buttons* (GI 50) [USA]
Hagiwara Sakutarō *Howling at the Moon: Poems and Prose*
(GI 57) [Japan]

2003
Rainer Maria Rilke *Duino Elegies* (GI 58) [Germany]
Paul Celan *Romanian Poems* (GI 81) [Romania]
Adonis *If Only the Sea Could Sleep* (GI 84) [Syria/Lebanon]
Henrik Nordbrandt *The Hangman's Lament* (GI 95) [Denmark]
Mario Luzi *Earthly and Heavenly Journey of Simone Martini*
(GI 99) [Italy]

2004

André Breton *Earthlight* (GI 102) [France]
Paul Celan *Breathturn* (GI 111) [Bukovina/France]
Paul Celan *Threadsuns* (GI 112) [Bukovina/France]
Paul Celan *Lightduress* (GI 113) [Bukovina/France]
Reina María Rodríguez *Violet Island and Other Poems* (GI 119) [Cuba]
Amelia Rosselli *War Variations* (GI 121) [Italy]

2005

Ko Un *Ten Thousand Lives* (GI 123) [Korea]
Vizar Zhiti *The Condemned Apple: Selected Poetry* (GI 134) [Albania]
Krzysztof Kamil Baczyński *White Magic and Other Poems* (GI 138) [Poland]
Gilbert Sorrentino *New and Selected Poems 1948-1998* (GI 143) [USA]

2006

Attila József *A Transparent Lion: Selected Poems* (GI 149) [Hungary]
Nishiwaki Janzuburō *A Modern Fable* (GI 151) [Japan]
Maurice Gilliams *The Bottle at Sea: The Complete Poems* (GI 153) [Belgium]
Takamuro Kōtarō *The Chieko Poems* (GI 160) [Japan]

GREEN INTEGER
Pataphysics and Pedantry

Douglas Messerli, *Publisher*

Essays, Manifestos, Statements, Speeches, Maxims,
Epistles, Diaristic Notes, Narratives, Natural Histories,
Poems, Plays, Performances, Ramblings, Revelations
and all such ephemera as may appear necessary
to bring society into a slight tremolo of confusion
and fright at least.

*

Individuals may order Green Integer titles through PayPal
(www.Paypal.com). Please pay the price listed below plus $2.00 for
postage to Green Integer through the PayPal system.
You can also visit our site at www.greeninteger.com
If you have questions please feel free to e-mail the publisher at
info@greeninteger.com
Bookstores and libraries should order through our distributors:
USA and Canada: Consortium Book Sales and Distribution
1045 Westgate Drive, Suite 90, Saint Paul, Minnesota 55114-1065
United Kingdom and Europe: Turnaround Publisher Services
Unit 3, Olympia Trading Estate, Coburg Road, Wood Green,
London N22 6TZ UK

*

±Adonis *If Only the Sea Could Sleep: Love Poems*
    [1-931243-29-8] $11.95
Hans Christian Andersen *Travels* [1-55713-344-1] $12.95
Eleanor Antin [Yevegeny Antiov] *The Man Without a World:*
    A Screenplay [1-892295-81-4] $10.95
Ingeborg Bachmann *Letters to Felician* [1-931243-16-6] $9.95
Krzysztof Kamil Baczyński *White Magic and Other Poems*
    [1-931243-81-6] $12.95
†Henri Bergson *Laughter: An Essay on the Meaning of the Comic*
    [1-899295-02-4] $11.95
Charles Bernstein *Republics of Reality: 1975-1995*
    [Sun & Moon Press: 1-55713-304-2] $14.95
        Shadowtime [1-933382-00-7] $11.95
André Breton   *Arcanum 17* [1-931243-27-1] $12.95
        *Earthlight [1-931243-27-1] $12.95
Lee Breuer *La Divina Caricatura* [1-931243-39-5] $14.95
Luis Buñuel *The Exterminating Angel* [1-931243-36-0] $11.95
Olivier Cadiot *Art Poetic'* [1-892295-22-9] $12.95
Francis Carco *Streetcorners: Prose Poems of the Demi-Monde*
    [1-931243-63-8] $12.95
Paul Celan *+Lightduress* [1-931243-75-1] $12.95
        Romanian Poems [1-892295-41-4] $10.95
        Threadsuns [1-931245-74-3] $12.95
Louis-Ferdinand Céline *Ballets without Music, without Dancers, without*
        Anything [1-892295-06-8] $10.95
        The Church: A Comedy in Five Acts
        [1-892295-78-4] $13.95
Andrée Chedid *Fugitive Suns: Selected Poetry* [1-892295-25-3] $11.95

Anton Chekhov *A Tragic Man Despite Himself: The Complete Short Plays* [1-931243-17-4] $24.95

Joseph Conrad *Heart of Darkness* [1-892295-49-0] $10.95

Charles Dickens *A Christmas Carol* [1-931243-18-2] $8.95

Mohammed Dib *L.A. Trip: A Novel in Verse* [1-931243-54-9] $11.95

Michael Disend *Stomping the Goyim* [1-9312243-10-7] $12.95

±José Donoso *Hell Has No Limits* [1-892295-14-8] $10.95

Oswald Egger *Room of Rumor: Tunings* [1-931243-66-2] $9.95

Andreas Embiricos *Amour Amour* [1-931243-26-3] $11.95

Ford Madox Ford *The Good Soldier* [1931243-62-x] $10.95

Jean Frémon •*Island of the Dead* [1-931243-31-x] $12.95

Sigmund Freud [with Wilhelm Jensen] *Gradiva* and *Delusion and Dream in Wilhelm Jensen's* Gradiva [1-892295-89-x] $13.95

Federico García Lorca *Suites* 1-892295-61-x] $12.95

Dieter M. Gräf *Tousled Beauty* [1-933382-01-5] $11.95

Elana Greenfield *Damascus Gate: Short Hallucinations* [1-931243-49-2] $10.95

Jean Grenier *Islands: Lyrical Essays* [1-892295-95-4] $12.95

Barbara Guest *The Confetti Trees* [Sun & Moon Press: 1-55713-390-5] $10.95

Hagiwara Sakutarō *Howling at the Moon: Poems and Prose* [1-931243-01-8] $11.95

Joshua Haigh [Douglas Messerli] *Letters from Hanusse* [1-892295-30-x] $12.95

†Knut Hamsun *The Last Joy* [1-931243-19-0] $12.95
On Overgrown Paths [1-892295-10-5] $12.95
A Wanderer Plays on Muted Strings [1-893395-73-3] $10.95

Sigurd Hoel *Meeting at the Milestone* [1-892295-31-8] $15.95

Wilhelm Jensen [with Sigmund Freud] *Gradiva* and *Delusion
          and Dream in Wilhelm Jensen's* Gradiva
          [1-893395-89-x] $12.95
Attila József *A Transparent Lion: Selected Poems* [1-933382-50-3] $12.95
James Joyce *On Ibsen* [1-55713-372-7] $8.95
Richard Kalich *Charlie P* [1-933382-05-8] $12.95
Ko Un *Ten Thousand Lives* [1-933382-06-6] $14.95
Else Lasker-Schüler *Selected Poems* [1-892295-86-5] $11.95
Mario Luzi *Earthly and Heavenly Journey of Simone Martini*
          [1-9312433-53-0] $14.95
†Thomas Mann **Six Early Stories* [1-892295-74-1] $10.95
†Harry Martinson *Views from a Tuft of Grass* [1-931243-78-6] $10.95
Julio Matas [with Carlos Felipe and Virgilio Piñera] *Three
          Masterpieces of Cuban Drama* [1-892295-66-0] $12.95
±Friederike Mayröcker *with each clouded peak* [Sun & Moon Press:
          1-55713-277-1] $11.95
Douglas Messerli *After* [Sun & Moon Press: 1-55713-353-0] $10.95
          Bow Down [ML&NLF: 1-928801-04-8] $12.95
          First Words [1-931243-41-7] $10.95
          ed. *Listen to the Mockingbird: American Folksongs and
          Popular Music Lyrics of the 19th Century*
          [1-892295-20-2] $13.95
          *Maxims from My Mother's Milk/Hymns to Him:
          A Dialogue* [Sun & Moon Press: 1-55713-047-7] $8.95
          [ed. with Mac Wellman] *From the Other Side of the
          Century: A New American Drama* 1960-1995
          [Sun & Moon Press: 1-55713-274-x] $29.95
          see also Joshua Haigh and Kier Peters
Vítězslav Nezval •*Antilyrik & Other Poems* [1-892295-75-x] $10.95
John O'Keefe *The Deatherians* [1-931243-50-6] $10.95

Kier Peters *A Dog Tries to Kiss the Sky: 7 Short Plays*
[1-931243-30-1] $12.95
The Confirmation [Sun & Moon Press: 1-55713-154-6] $6.95
Pedro Pietri *The Masses Are Asses* [1-892295-62-8] $8.95
Edgar Allan Poe *Eureka, A Prose Poem* [1-55713-329-8] $10.95
Jean Renoir *An Interview* [1-55713-330-1] $9.95
Rainer Maria Rilke *Duino Elegies* [1-931243-07-7] $10.95
Reina María Rodríguez *Violet Island and Other Poems*
[1-892295-65-2] $12.95
Martha Ronk *Displeasures of the Table* [1-892295-44-x] $9.95
Joe Ross *EQUATIONS=equals* [1-931243-61-1] $10.95
Amelia Rosselli *War Variations* [1-931243-55-7] $14.95
Arno Schmidt *Radio Dialogs I* [1-892295-01-6] $12.95
Radio Dialogs II [1-892295-80-6] $13.95
The School for Atheists: A Novella=Comedy in 6 Acts
[1-892295-96-2] $16.95
Arthur Schnitzler *Dream Story* [1-931243-48-4] $11.95
Lieutenant Gustl [1-931243-46-8] $9.95
Eleni Sikelianos *The Monster Lives of Boys and Girls*
[1-931243-67-0] $10.95
Gilbert Sorrentino *Gold Fools* [1-892295-67-9] $14.95
New and Selected Poems 1958-1998
[1-892295-82-2] $14.95
Thorvald Steen *Don Carlos* and *Giovanni* [1-931243-79-4] $14.95
Gertrude Stein *History, or Messages from History* [1-55713-354-9] $5.95
Mexico: A Play [1-892295-36-9] $5.95
Tender Buttons [1-931243-42-5] $10.95
Three Lives [1-892295-33-4] $12.95
To Do: A Book of Alphabets and Birthdays
[1-892295-16-4] $9.95
Cole Swensen *Noon* [1-931243-58-1] $10.95

Henry David Thoreau *Civil Disobediance* [1-892295-93-8] $6.95

Mark Twain [Samuel Clemens] *What Is Man?* [1-892295-15-6] $10.95

Paul Verlaine *The Cursed Poets* [1-931243-15-8] $11.95

Mark Wallace *Temporary Worker Rides a Subway*
        [1-931243-60-3] $10.95

Mac Wellman *Crowtet 1: A Murder of Crows and The Hyacinth Macaw*
        [1-892295-52-0] $11.95

    Crowtet 2: Second-Hand Smoke and The Lesser Magoo
        [1-931243-71-9] $12.95

    The Land Beyond the Forest: Dracula and Swoop
        [Sun & Moon Press: 1-55713-228-3] $12.95

Oscar Wilde *The Critic As Artist* [1-55713-328-x] $9.95

William Carlos Williams *The Great American Novel*
              [1-931243-52-2] $10.95

Yang Lian *Yi* [1-892295-68-7] $14.95

Yi Ch'ŏngjun *Your Paradise* [1-931243-69-7] $13.95

Visar Zhiti *The Condemned Apple: Selected Poetry*
        [1-931243-72-7] $10.95

† Author winner of the Nobel Prize for Literature

± Author winner of the America Award for Literature

• Book translation winner of the PEN American Center
  Translation Award [PEN-West]

* Book translation winner of the PEN/Book-of-the-Month Club
  Translation Prize

+ Book translation winner of the PEN Award for Poetry in Translation

The America Awards

FOR A LIFETIME CONTRIBUTION TO INTERNATIONAL WRITING
Awarded by the Contemporary Arts Educational Project, Inc.
in loving memory of Anna Fahrni

The 2006 Award winner is:

JULIEN GRACQ (LOUIS POIRIER)

[FRANCE] 1910

Previous winners:

1994 AIMÉ CESAIRE [Martinique] 1913
1995 HAROLD PINTER [England] 1930
1996 JOSÉ DONOSO [Chile] 1924-1996 (awarded prior to his death)
1997 FRIEDERIKE MAYRÖCKER [Austria] 1924
1998 RAFAEL ALBERTI [Spain] 1902-1998 (awarded prior to his death)
1999 JACQUES ROUBAUD [France] 1932
2000 EUDORA WELTY [USA] 1909-2001
2001 INGER CHRISTENSEN [Denmark] 1935
2002 PETER HANDKE [Austria] 1942
2003 ADONIS [Syria/Lebanon] 1930
2004 JOSÉ SARAMAGO [Portugal] 1922
2005 ANDREA ZANZOTTO [Italy] 1921

The rotating panel for The America Awards currently consists of Douglas Messerli [chairman], Will Alexander, Luigi Ballerini, Peter Constantine, Peter Glassgold, Deborah Meadows, Martin Nakell, John O'Brien, Marjorie Perloff, Joe Ross, Jerome Rothenberg, Paul Vangelisti, and Mac Wellman.